Christian

Welcome
Home

Belonging to the Church

by
Dwight Longenecker

*All booklets are published thanks to the
generous support of the members of the
Catholic Truth Society*

CATHOLIC TRUTH SOCIETY
PUBLISHERS TO THE HOLY SEE

Contents

1. The Family of God

The Homecoming

One of the most famous stories Jesus Christ told was about a runaway son. The boy went to his wealthy father and asked for his inheritance money

early. The doting father gave him some cash and the boy ran off and wasted the money on parties and pleasure.

When the money ran out the boy's friends ran out too. Hard times hit the city and soon the boy was stuck with no money, no friends, no qualifications and no future.

He ended up taking a job as a pig farmer, and had to fight the pigs for enough food to eat. Then he remembered his father.

At that point Jesus says the boy 'came to himself.' He saw himself and his circumstances as they really were. He realised how good he'd had it at home. Even his father's servants were better off than he was. If he were to go home and volunteer to be a servant in his father's house perhaps he would at least have a decent meal every day.

The boy started on the long road home. As he approached he saw that his father was at the front gate waiting and watching for his return. The father rejoiced at his son's return, forgave him everything and welcomed him home with a great homecoming feast.

When a person decides to change their life and follow God's way instead of their own selfish way through life it is just like the homecoming of that runaway son. Every time we take a step towards God and away from our own selfishness it is as if we have arrived home. Part of us is complete. A deep dark corner of our lives is touched with light and we begin to glimpse the possibility of finding the peace we have always looked for.

Brothers and Sisters Abounding

One of the first Christian leaders named Paul said that to come home like this was to become a member of the family of God. He recognised that all those who follow Jesus Christ are the fugitive sons and daughters of God, and that to be restored to the family we first have to turn towards home.

This is a reality, not just a theory or a nice way of talking about being religious. Once we turn from our way and accept Christ's way; once we believe that Jesus

Christ died to give us new life, a real transformation takes place in our relationship with God. Like runaways we have come home, and the father welcomes us with open arms. As the father did in the story, God then gives us a whole array of good gifts.

This new relationship with God means we are also in a new relationship with every other person who has ever followed Jesus Christ down through the centuries. For two thousand years people have taken the same decision. They too have realised that Jesus Christ died for them. They have also decided to leave everything and follow him. Each in their own way have also returned home and been welcomed into the family of God.

The Christians down through the ages are therefore our brothers and sisters. They are not alive on this earth, but they are alive on the other side, and they are interested in us and the rest of God's family. These people who have been totally transformed by Christ's loving power are the saints. In Christ they are our older brothers and sisters.

Making New Old Friends

The saints make up a vast and varied collection of people. There are saints from every walk of life, from every class, race and nationality. Children, old people, soldiers, nuns, politicians and priests have all become saints. Parents, husbands and wives, scholars and simpletons, princes and peasants have all become saints. The vast array of saints shows us that anyone can be totally transformed by Christ if they are willing.

The Bible calls the saints a 'great cloud of witnesses'. The word for 'witness' is actually 'martyr', and in their own way every saint has learned to give up their life for Christ. Some of them literally gave up their lives at the hands of violent men. Others gave up their lives in the slow service of others and in a life made long by the hardship of constant self-giving.

The saints still work with Christ for the redemption of the world even though they are in heaven, not on earth. As we fight the battle against evil we become aware that we do not fight alone. Our older brothers and sisters in the faith love us and fight with us in the great battle.

As we begin walking in the Christian life it will not be long before we learn more about certain saints. Their lives will appeal to us. We will want to learn more about how they followed Christ, and we will desire to follow their example. As we do we will feel that the saints are with us as friends and fellow travellers in the journey.

Unity and Diversity

We can't see the saints, but we know they are with us. They are present during our prayers. They are present at the Mass, where we recognise their presence and pray with them. They are present with us as we meditate and contemplate. We soon become aware that we do not worship alone, but we worship with a great cloud of witnesses surrounding us.

I mention the saints in heaven first because it is vital to remember that being a Christian joins us with a group of people who have been alive and active in the world for the last two thousand years. What we do here and now is connected with what has gone before. What we do here and now has grown from their Christ-filled lives before us.

Once we are aware of our relationship with all the saints of the past we will better understand our relationship with all the other Christians in the present. When we become Catholic we do not simply join our local church. The Catholic Church is vast, and there is a huge variety of people and types of people within it all over the world. Just as there is a huge variety of saints, so there is a huge range of people who are Catholics in the world today.

Within the vast range of national groups, races, classes and abilities there is a remarkable unity.

Down through the ages kings, tyrants, political parties and pressure groups have tried to establish world wide power. They have tried to set up an empire, political network or universal brotherhood that included all people. In the Catholic Church it already exists. Within the Church all people can exist together as brothers and sisters in Christ.

When you join the Church, therefore, you immediately become one with all other Catholics around the world no matter what their language, race, nationality, gender, class or background. This range of personalities and types are found not only as you travel around the world, but in your own local parish. There at Mass on a Sunday you will also find a vast background of different types of people. It is vitally important to belong to this varied group of people in the local parish, because that is where you connect with the wider Catholic Church.

Groups and Sub Groups

Because of the vast range of people in a local parish it is sometimes difficult to feel at home. A Catholic church sometimes feels more like a bus stop than a family gathering. In other words, it feels like this vast range of people have gathered together for the same practical reason, but otherwise they don't seem to belong together at all.

It is vital to take an active part in our local parish because that is where we learn to get on with other Catholics who may be very different from us. But it is also important to realise that within the Catholic Church there are many smaller groups and sub-groups. If the Catholic Church is like a huge tree, then there are many different branches and twigs. Along with active parish involvement many Catholics also find a group or sub group within the church where they find others with shared interests and outlooks.

The varied groups and sub groups focus on different activities within the whole Church community. There are charities that are involved in helping others in the local community, as well as at the national and international levels. There are political pressure groups if you go for that sort of thing. There are groups for young people and groups for the elderly.

Some groups nurture prayer, spirituality, Christian growth and evangelisation. Others focus on worship, music and the liturgy. Some help build marriages and family life. Others are involved in education, health care, ecology and concern for the poor. Still others look after children, foster adoption and work to eliminate the crime of abortion. All these groups are Catholic. Some of them are well established. Others are exciting new movements in the Church. All of them focus on Jesus Christ in the Catholic Church, but they also have their own priorities, aims and ways of working.

Finding Your Place

To fit into the family of God it might take some time to find the right group or sub group to belong to. You must know what interests you and where you will fit in best. The easiest way to discover the way forward is to follow what you find attractive within the church.

Parish life is where the ordinary day to day spiritual life takes place. Seeking out one of the groups within the Catholic Church will help you feel at home. It will provide a way for your spiritual life to go forward in leaps and bounds. The others in that group will help you to feel part of the larger family, and as you get involved with them in the life of Christ you will realise that this kind of unity and commitment is what makes life worthwhile.

As you discover the Catholic Church you will find a spiritual way forward that is right for you, but you will also find many opinions and ways that don't suit you. If you happen to be conservative by nature you will find plenty of liberals in the church. If you are liberally minded you will have to put up with plenty of conservatives. If you are introspective you will have come across extroverted people, and vice versa.

The same holds true for every other area of taste and temperament. Not everyone will find the music or worship in their church to their taste. There will be people in the church you disagree with or dislike. There will be others who dislike and disagree with you. This is all part of belonging to the great family of God called the Catholic Church. It is the same with every large family. We have to learn to get on with one another, be tolerant and learn from those with whom we disagree.

Fitting In, Not Sticking Out

It will not always be easy to stay with the Catholic Church. Sometimes other churches will seem more attractive and happier places to be. But joining the Catholic Church is a serious business. It is like marriage. You make the promises for better or for worse. It is no good flitting from one church to another any more than it is a good idea to flit from one marriage to another.

Throughout one's relationship with the church the difficulties are actually part of the larger test. The restless person constantly runs from one church to another, always thinking that they know what is best for themselves spiritually. The mature person buckles down to the difficult business of finding God within the Church even when that church is not always to their liking. This means they will stick with their local parish church even if everything there is not totally to their taste.

This process actually helps us to grow spiritually. To be a Catholic means we accept that the church is bigger, older and wiser than we are. It means we are not changing the church, but allowing the church to change us. The Church was there before we were. Therefore we should try to adapt ourselves to the church. We shouldn't expect the church to adapt to us.

Finding our place in the church is a necessity because the whole point of the Christian life is to go with God. By fitting into our place in church we put our own will on one side. We try to be humble and say, 'Well, maybe I don't know best all the time. I'm going to try to learn from the difficulty. I'm

going to find God right here - not somewhere else.'
At that point we start to learn that God is best
discovered by finding our rightful place within the
vast and beautiful unity that is the One, Holy,
Catholic and Apostolic Church.

2. The One Church

One of the things that makes us frustrated and angry is chaos and disorder. It is part of human nature to want things to fit together. We want to find meaning in the universe. We want all that is broken to be mended; all that is wounded to be healed and all that is divided to be reconciled. In other words, we want unity.

The desires of our body war against the better ideals of our soul. Our worldly ambitions clash with our spiritual goals. Our mental ideas and viewpoint don't fit the reality of life. Within ourselves we long for unity.

We also long for unity in our relationships. We want our families and friends to live together in peace and harmony, not in rebellion, anger, revenge and violence. We also long for unity in our communities, our nation and our world. We don't want the destruction of war, violence, hatred and selfishness.

This longing for unity reaches to the whole world. We want a system of belief that reconciles not only us, our friends and our relationships, but the whole world. We sense that the world is divided and that various elements are at war with one another and wish for true peace, harmony and unity to prevail. When we say that we believe in 'one Church' we profess our belief that the unity we long for exists in the Christian Church. That unity is not perfect yet, but in the Church we can get a glimpse of the unity that all human beings should share.

One Lord, One Faith, One Baptism

In the New Testament the Christian leader Paul said, 'There is one Body, one Spirit, one Lord, one faith, one baptism,' When we are baptised we enter into that one Body. We trust that one faith, and join our divided selves with this greater unity that exists within God's will. Elsewhere Paul said the Church is the Body of Christ, and that each member is a cell of that body. Jesus himself said there would be 'one flock and one shepherd.'

Jesus wanted there to be one church on earth. That church was meant to be a source of reconciliation, unity and peace for the whole of humanity. As individuals come into unity with Christ they were also to come into unity with one another, and with God's plan for the whole world. This unity is a vital sign that Jesus' message is true. Jesus prayed that his followers would be one as he and the Father are one. This unity had to be visible unity because Jesus said others would see that unity and believe in him.

The Church is not just a club of like minded religious people. It is actually a unified, coherent and consistent body of people. It has a life of its own down through the ages. It is almost as if the church is a living organism with its own mind and spirit and soul.

That organism is united in the one faith that was given to her by Jesus Christ. Each member of the organism is united by the fact that they share that faith and have been baptised into the new life of Jesus Christ. Each member everywhere in the world, from every race, language, tribe and tradition is united by their shared allegiance to Jesus Christ as their Lord and God. This unity is not just a pretty word picture. It is a reality. This means I am not alone. I am a part of every other Christian I meet. I am not an island. I am a living cell in the great, cosmic, body of Christ on earth.

Eastern Orthodox

All Christians are united by our shared faith in Jesus Christ, and our baptism into his death and resurrection. This is a real and permanent unity that can never be destroyed. However, if the Church is the body of Christ, that body is wounded by division and strife. Not only is the body wounded; it still bleeds.

During the first thousand years of the Christian faith the Church really was united. There were some breakaway groups down though the centuries. There were little groups that disagreed and separated themselves from the mainstream, but for the most part the Christian Church was united around a group of leaders with the Bishop of Rome as the recognised head.

The Church's life was closely bound up with the political life of the Roman Empire, and as the Roman Empire crumbled and was divided, the Christian Church also fell into opposing camps. Increasingly, the churches in the ancient Middle East and North Africa went their own way. Nevertheless, unity was retained under the leadership of the Bishop of Rome.

Then at about the turn of the first millennium the conflict between the Eastern Churches in Greece, Turkey, the Middle East and North Africa came to a head. They broke away from the ancient leadership of Rome. The Roman leaders and the Eastern Church leaders cut each other off and a huge division in the Church took place. For complicated reasons the division still exists. Christians from the East - including

Russia and parts of Eastern Europe - are partially cut off from the rest of the Catholic Church.

We look to the Eastern Christians and admire them as our brothers and sisters in Christ. Like Catholics, they have retained the ancient faith that has been handed down to us from the first followers of Jesus called apostles. The Eastern Churches have retained wonderful traditions and have endured terrible persecution. Catholics long for a reunion to take place so that the whole Church may once again breathe with two lungs of East and West.

Christ longs for the church to be one, and we must work together in every way with the Eastern Christians to heal this ancient division so that we can work together to do Christ's will in the world.

Reformation Churches

Five hundred years after the Eastern and Western parts of the Christian church divided, another terrible division in the Church took place. In the sixteenth century Europe was going through a time of enormous social and technological upheaval. At the same time the church system that had survived for fifteen hundred years was beginning to show its age. In some parts of the church there was corruption, complacency and confusion.

In the midst of this confusion came a new teaching that seemed to liberate individual Christians. The printing press had just been invented and ordinary people were learning to read. They wanted to read the Bible, and what they found there was a simple gospel message that seemed divorced from the rich, ornate church led by wealthy bishops, priests and monks.

Fiery preachers stirred the people up and called for change. Unfortunately, the church was unable to change quickly enough. Those calling for reform couldn't wait. At the same time new political forces were rising in Europe. The new religious thinkers joined forces with the new political leaders and before long they had the power, influence and support to start their own churches.

In Germany the Lutherans broke away from the ancient church. In Switzerland the Calvinists (or Presbyterians) broke away. In England the Church of England had already been founded. There were many other smaller groups as well. Each religious teacher seemed to find something different in the Bible and ultimately they disagreed with one another and set out to start their own churches.

Now a directory of denominations in the USA lists over 20,000 different non-Catholic denominations.

Surely this is not what Christ intended when he founded one Church to reconcile all people and bring everyone into a new kind of unity for mankind.

A Wounded Church

It cannot be overestimated how much damage this division has caused the Church of Christ. The battle against evil is much more difficult if the soldiers of goodness are divided among themselves.

One of the things that must put anyone off becoming a Christian is the unseemly fighting between different Christian groups. When Catholics and Eastern Orthodox kill one another; when Protestants and Catholics fight to the death the whole message of Christ is trampled in the mud and Christ's body is wounded deeply in a fresh and terrible way.

Catholics believe that all Christians who have faith in Christ and are baptised are in a real and substantial unity with them. However, they also recognise that the unity of Christ's Church is deeply wounded. Furthermore, the grievances of the past cannot be glossed over. We cannot simply pretend the problem does not exist.

Because Catholics and other Christians are not fully united we cannot share in the fullness of Holy Communion with other Christians.

Communion is a sign of the unity we share as Catholic Christians. To share openly in the fullness of communion with non-Catholics is to lie publicly. It is to say that a communion exists between us that does not, in fact, exist.

When we honestly face the division in this way it hurts Catholics as much as anyone else. To do so we are not judging the goodness of other Christians. We are simply saying that real divisions still exist and problems do not go away by pretending they don't exist. Instead Catholics are committed to working together with our separated brothers and sisters to solve the problems of a wounded church through dialogue, self sacrifice, forgiveness and optimism for the future.

Working Towards Unity

The best way to attain unity in the Church of Christ is for individuals to join themselves with the one church that is the most ancient, the biggest, the most authoritative and the most unified. This is the Catholic Church. No other church or denomination can claim to be one as the Catholic Church is one.

Then as a Catholic it is important to work together with other Christians as much as possible in the fight against evil. It is possible to work together with non-

Catholic Christians in the areas of spreading the good news, charity work, political involvement, social concerns and regular prayer and worship.

On the formal level the Catholic Church is involved in complicated discussions with a whole range of non-Catholic Christians. Great progress is being made in resolving differences, clearing up misunderstandings and developing new trust and friendship.

The same is possible on the local and personal level. There is simply no room for Christians of various traditions to be suspicious of one another. Fighting and quarrelling amongst ourselves is a victory for the forces of evil. All of us who follow Christ are called to unity with him and unity with one another. The fact that this unity has been broken only calls for us to work harder to love and understand one another. Only in that way can we all attain to the radiant goodness and the abundant life that Jesus Christ has to offer.

3. The Holy Church

All of us are divided personalities. We are confused about what we really want. Our worst desires battle with our best ambitions. Our shadow self is at war with the part of us that wants the very best. The closer a person gets to resolving this inner conflict, the more mature, whole and fulfilled he becomes.

A mature and whole person has realised that his or her shadow side is a distorted part of their good side. Each negative part of us is only the dark side of a genuine strength. The mature person learns how to turn stubbornness into determination, lust into love, ambition into positive power and greed into a desire for goodness.

This is what holiness is like. In fact the word 'holiness' is linked to the word 'wholeness'. When a person is holy he or she is whole. They are complete, mature, fully formed. He or she is all that they possibly could be. The warring elements in their nature have been reconciled. Priorities have been established and that person has learned to live at peace with himself, with God and with everyone else.

Amazing Grace

Jesus Christ was perfectly human in this way. He not only reveals the fullness of God, but he also reveals the full potential of humanity. When we follow Christ we do not simply seek to follow his teaching. We actually want to be like him. We want to be transformed into 'little Christs'. He was the perfectly whole person, and we want to be as perfectly whole and unified as he was.

The difference between the Christian faith and a self help programme is that Christians admit the fact that they cannot make this transformation happen on their own. We might be able to lose weight, give up smoking or exercise more through will power, but a real lasting inner transformation of our whole personalities is more than we can manage.

Real, lasting inner change is impossible to accomplish on our own for two reasons. First, we cannot manage this sort of change because we have so many blind spots about our own faults. How can we change if we honestly cannot see the things that need to be changed?

Second, we cannot change on our own because we do not have the power to change ourselves. The power to really be transformed can only be the power that made us in the first place, and we do not control that power. God does. Christians therefore ask for God to transform us by his special power.

'Grace' is the power of God at work in our lives to transform us into all that he wants us to be. Grace is available to us free for the asking. If we ask for the grace to change, God really does enter our lives and transform us. Grace comes to us in many ways, but it is most present to us through the life and ministry of the Church.

The Power of Perfection

We say the Church is 'holy' not because everyone in it is perfectly saintly all the time. Anybody can see that isn't true. Instead we proclaim that the Church is holy because God's powerful grace is present in and through the Church at all times. This grace imbues the church with a goodness and a power that is greater than the imperfections it is trying to overcome.

God's grace ministers to us through the church as a mother helps, nurtures and instructs her child. The child might be weak, but the mother's love is strong. We need that powerful force of goodness in our lives if we are to become like Christ. Without it we are simply trying hard to be nicer better people, and we won't really get that far. So one wise writer observed that 'it is impossible to have God as your father if you do not have the Church as your mother.'

Because the Church is like a mother to us we sometimes compare the Church to Jesus' mother Mary. Mary was a perfectly whole and complete person. She was holy in a natural, wise and loving way. As she is the image of the perfectly loving and gentle mother, so she is also the image of the Church. As she nurtured Jesus, the Christian community becomes our teacher, our comforter, and our friend. As a mother the Church feeds us, supports us and gives us a spiritual home.

As we receive God's grace within the Church we take great strides towards that wholeness which is called holiness. The person who is perfectly whole and complete in this way is a person of great power. God radiates through their life in an amazingly potent way. They can do great things. They can change the world. They can move mountains of resistance and difficulty. When we say the Church is 'holy' we mean the church empowers people like this.

The Problem of Imperfection

But if you know anything about the Church you will protest, 'Hold on a moment! The Christians I know aren't anything like that. They're a grumpy, narrow minded group of people who are always fighting amongst themselves.'

We should be willing to excuse the little imperfections of ordinary Christians. After all, nobody said they would be perfect all at once. All of us are on a steep learning curve. We're still taking the lessons and doing the practice. We might be on the right road, but we admit that we haven't arrived yet.

Little imperfections are one thing, but what about the huge crimes committed by Christians - especially those committed by Christian leaders? What are we to make of paedophile priests, IRA murderers, abusive nuns and power hungry popes? What can we say about wars, imprisonment, torture, and executions conducted in the name of Christ?

There are two answers to the problem of imperfection amongst Christians. First, it is fair to remember that there is a war going on. There are forces that will do anything to destroy Christ and his Church. These powers will use the media to twist the truth and make problems worse than they are. To be fair we must read both sides of any story and really gather facts - not just propaganda. When we look at the facts fairly the wrongdoing is often not as bad as the propaganda would make out.

Nevertheless, there have been some monstrous crimes committed by Christians - both lay people and high-ranking Christian leaders. It would be foolish to suppose otherwise. All we can say is that such crimes are not only terrible, but they are made worse because the person has professed to follow Jesus Christ.

Don't Forget the War

But are you really surprised when good people do bad things? Good people are those who are most involved in the battle against evil, and in any war there will be some major casualties. Sometimes the enemy will win a major battle even though he will never win the war.

While God's grace is at work, human selfishness, greed, anger and violence are also still at work. The war between good and evil is always present, and when you think about it, where else would the war claim the most casualties but on the front line - within the army of those most committed to goodness, truth and light. Isn't that where the wounds will be most nasty and the casualties most horrific?

There is no excuse for the wrong done by religious people, but once we see that the war is still going on, the wrongdoing becomes more understandable and forgivable. It is possible to condemn the crimes of Christians but still admit the truth of their message. When a person doesn't live up to the ideal it doesn't mean the ideal was wrong.

Finally, when we see the great crimes of men and women who professed to be good should we really be surprised? We mustn't excuse the wrongdoing, but did we really think that all Christians were going to be squeaky clean and victorious all the time? Wouldn't you be suspicious if the history of the Church were one hundred percent perfect? If it were it wouldn't be real.

Seeing What Can Be

Furthermore, whenever we pick out the bad things Christians have done we have to be fair and also see the good things that many Christians have accomplished. For every paedophile priest there are one hundred who live selfless lives of service to their people. For every corrupt pope there have been hundreds of hard working, self-sacrificing and holy popes and bishops.

When we say that the Church is 'holy' we are not saying that everybody within it has been perfect all the time. Far from it. Instead we mean that the Church's holiness is real even though it is soiled by sin. The Church is holy because she is on a holy mission. She is fighting the good fight, and she is filled with the Holy Spirit to enable that fight to go on.

A mature person is neither a total pessimist nor a naive optimist. Instead the whole person sees the whole picture. They see how things really are, but they also see how things can be. They see the real faults in themselves, in others and in the world, but they also see the great potential in themselves, in others and in the world.

The Church is holy in this sense because she helps us see both what we are and what we can be. The Church doesn't whitewash the human condition. She says bluntly, 'We are all sinners. We are lost in the dark and need someone to rescue us.' But the Church also says, 'We are all sons and daughters of the living God. We were created to be no less than the radiant inhabitants of heaven. Let us be all that we can be in the power of God, leaving behind the works of darkness and moving forward together into the full and abundant life that he has promised.'

Even Now, Not Yet

There are two dimensions to this full and abundant life. The crimes of Christians and the divisions in the Church remind us that life here on earth is anything but the perfection that is promised. But on the other hand, the Church helps us to see in a very real sense that full and abundant life is a reality right here and now.

The holiness or 'wholeness' that Christ promises is a reality even if that reality is imperfectly realised here on earth. In all sorts of ways we can experience the reality of this full and abundant life. In our own lives, in our families, in our communities, in our churches, in our nation and in our world there are plenty of times when people really do come together and achieve the unity and peace that we all long for.

In moments of prayer and worship, in times of friendship and love, in experiences and interests that unite us like sport, music and art we transcend our differences and reach toward that reconciliation, peace, and unity that marks the abundant life.

The highlight of all these experiences is to come together each week at Mass. Together with a whole range of different personality types, social classes, nationalities and races we come to worship

God. In this shared focus we express the one-ness and holiness that all of us are striving for - even though we realise that we have not yet attained it in all its fullness.

4. The Catholic Church

If you want to discover the reality of the Catholic Church don't travel to Rome. That is simply where the international headquarters are located. Instead discover your local Catholic parish church. There in your own town the one universal community of Christ's disciples has its local branch.

I should warn you that when you go to the local Catholic Church you will not find the perfect church. There will be problems. You might find the services difficult to follow at first. You may discover that the people are not very friendly and don't seem to care if you have just joined. When you get to know the people you will find that they have plenty of faults. (In other words, they are just like you).

A person does not join the Catholic Church because it is the church with the best music or the nicest people or the most interesting sermons. To tell you the truth, if you want nice music go to a concert. If you want nice people join the country club. If you want good speeches join a speaker's club. But if you want to belong to the fullest expression of the Body of Christ on earth, then become a Catholic.

Your local Catholic parish is where the ancient, universal Church that Christ founded becomes real. There you will meet real people who are struggling to fight the battle against evil and who are also seeking to follow Christ. Just as marriage makes love real, so joining the Catholic Church makes a commitment to Christ real. When something is real it is both difficult and glorious. So it is with marriage and with being a Catholic. It is tough. It is a challenge. But then, did you expect the Christian life to be easy?

Here There and Everywhere

The word 'Catholic' means 'universal'. In other words, the Catholic Church is everywhere. Over the centuries, by the power of the Holy Spirit, the Catholic community has permeated into every continent, land and country. People have become Catholics from virtually every tribe, nationality and race.

As a result, there is a huge variety within the Catholic Church. If you go to South America or Africa you will find poor Catholics living in simple core communities. They might worship in a church that is no more than a shed. Their music will be simple ethnic music and their prayers will be the prayers of the poor.

On the other hand, if you visit an affluent suburb in the United States or Europe you will find wealthy Catholics who are struggling with the difficulties of being rich. How is it possible for them to follow Christ when they have so much material wealth? They might worship in posh churches with large budgets, but we shouldn't judge by appearances. It might be that they are giving away a large proportion of their money to help their poor brothers and sisters on the other side of the world.

Contrasts like these can be multiplied over and over again. East and West, North and South, rich and poor, educated and uneducated, black and white, men and women, old people and children - in the Catholic Church they all exist together as the family of God.

Believing in a universal church does not only mean we believe with our heads that such a world wide family exists; it also means that we believe with our hearts that we belong to that family. It means that we become a living part of the whole complex, fascinating and vast community of followers of Jesus Christ around the world and down the ages.

Salvation outside the Church?

It is a wonderful thing to belong to a family of people who are united in one faith, following one

Lord and belonging to one church. The great power of the Catholic Church is that it joins together this great company of believers from every background imaginable.

Membership in this body does not simply mean that we are part of a world wide club with more members than any other organisation. Being a Catholic also means that we are members of the Body of Christ. As such we have a new power in our lives. We share in the same power that raised Jesus from the dead. Because we share in this power we are delivered from eternal death. This salvation from death is guaranteed to all who follow Christ and who remain in his way of love and truth.

Isn't that unfair on all those who are not Catholics? In the section on 'one Church' I explained that all non-Catholic Christians who have faith in Christ, and who have been baptised into his death and resurrection, also share in the hope of salvation. But there are many people who follow religions other than Christianity. Are they able to be saved or will they experience eternal death?

There is also the question of all those who have never heard about Jesus Christ. Will God send them all to hell simply because they have never had the chance to have faith in Christ and be baptised? If so, it sounds very unfair.

Denial and Affirmation

Catholics recognise the goodness and truth in other religions. We don't determine the eternal destiny of anyone. That is for God to do. We recognise that the Jews, for example, are our older brothers and sisters in the faith. Jesus was a Jew. Christianity grew out of the Jewish religion. Catholics believe that a Jewish person's faith would be fulfilled and completed if he or she were to become a Christian, but we also recognise that God can draw faithful Jews to himself if it is his will. If he does so it is through Jesus Christ's victory over death.

Catholics also recognise that Muslims seek to follow the same God as Christians and Jews. Muslims follow the teachings of the prophet Mohammed as written in the Koran. We don't agree with everything they teach, and they certainly don't agree with everything that Catholics believe. However, despite our disagreements, there is much that we can agree on, and there is much that we can praise within the Islamic religion. Catholics are able to affirm these good things in other religions without denying the truth they hold to as Catholics. We can also admit that a good faithful Muslim may be closer to heaven than an unfaithful Catholic.

In the end God is the one who decides if someone is saved from death. We do know that God is not willing for anyone to perish forever. We know that God sent Jesus not to condemn the world, but to save the world. We pray that through Jesus' death and resurrection all people might be saved, and we trust God to answer this prayer in his own way.

Us and Them

Christianity remains the largest world religion, but there are many other religions besides the Muslims and Jews. One can see how a Muslim or a Jew, who claims to worship the same God as Christians, might be closer to Christianity than people of other faiths.

You might wonder what happens to Buddhists, Sikhs, Bahai's, Hindus, pagans, animists, etc. etc. They don't profess to worship the same God as the Christians. In the gospel Jesus says clearly that he is the only way to God the Father. If those who follow other religions do not believe in Jesus can they be saved?

Once again, Catholics believe in goodness, truth and beauty wherever it is found. It is easy to recognise truth, goodness and beauty in every world religion. Catholics do not believe that all other religions are one hundred percent wrong. Instead we believe that the other world religions are good as far as they go, but that they are only ever a preparation for the fullness for God's truth as shown in Jesus Christ. In the other religions the truth is understood in partial way. In Jesus Christ the truth has come in all its fullness.

As a result, it is possible for a person of some other faith to follow their religion in all sincerity and to find the salvation that is won for them through Jesus Christ. If they follow the truth, goodness and beauty that they have with a passionate and faithful heart, then they are, as much as they are able, following Jesus Christ who is the very incarnation of goodness, truth and beauty.

A Universal Mission

The Catholic Church is the Universal Church, and that means that she has a universal mission. Before he went back to heaven Jesus commanded his followers to go into the whole world to proclaim the good news. He wanted everyone to be set free from their selfishness to attain a new and abundant life.

Catholics want to learn from non-Christian religions. We want to claim what is good in them and endorse all that is true and beautiful in their teachings. However, we are also aware that the Catholic system is the only one that is truly universal. In other words, all that is good, beautiful and true within all the other religions can also be found within the Catholic faith.

If you knew someone who was digging a trench with a teaspoon you might applaud his efforts. You could acknowledge that he was doing an excellent job as far as his skill and his tools could allow. But if you had a spade or a bulldozer you would want to tell him about the even better tools that you had available, so that he could dig a better ditch in a fraction of the time.

This is how Catholics feel about Jesus' command to tell others the good news. For those who have never heard the news, the commandment is simple: tell everyone that God loves them and Jesus has come to set them free from selfishness and final death.

For those who follow other religions the process is like telling the person who is using a teaspoon to dig a ditch that there is a fuller, better, quicker and happier way to complete the same task.

Redeeming the Whole World

This is why the Catholic Church will always be a missionary church. Every Catholic - whether they are an ordinary person or a priest, bishop, monk or nun are called to tell others the good news about Jesus Christ.

Our mission is to do nothing less than transform the world. Jesus died and rose again to bring the power to effect that transformation. We, as his Body on earth today are required to carry on his work and complete the job he gave us to do.

Each of us must get on with the job in the way best suited to our own personalities, gifts and abilities. Some will help to redeem the world by telling people about Jesus Christ and helping them to have faith and come to be baptised.

Others will be busy transforming the world through political activity, or through education, health care or social work. Others transform the world by bringing up many children who are on fire with the love of God. Still others will work to transform the whole world by giving their lives to prayer and worship.

No matter what our particular task each one of us is called to transform the world by first of all being transformed ourselves. Do you want others to know the joy, power and confidence that comes from having faith in Christ? Then show them the proof in your own transformed life.

The command to go out into the world and transform it by his power was the last word Jesus gave to his apostles. They bore his word and his power into the world, and we take part in the same mission because we share in the same faith that has been given to us by those very same apostles two thousand years ago.

5. The Apostolic Church

Jesus told a story about two men who built houses. The first man found a cheap piece of sandy ground and put up a nice house quite easily.

The second man invested in a rocky piece of high ground. It was hard work to build the house in such a place, but the foundations were firm and sure. When the floods and rains came the man who built on sand saw his house fall down while the man who built on rock was safe and secure.

Later in the New Testament Saint Paul says that the Church is built on the foundation of the prophets and apostles. What he means is that the community of Christians is like the second man's house. It is built carefully and with much hard work on a solid and sure foundation. As Christians our belief, our worship and our work is rooted in the teachings of the Jewish religion and the life and ministry of Jesus' first followers.

Jesus had many followers or disciples, but from them he chose twelve for a special ministry of leadership. These twelve are called 'apostles' which means 'ambassadors' or 'sent ones.' Jesus gave the apostles authority to continue his work. He said that he was sending them as God had sent him into the world. He also promised to be with them forever, and to send the Holy Spirit to guide and strengthen them.

Therefore, when Jesus left this world he left behind a group of men who would be his agents. As he was the hand of God, they would be his hands, his feet, his voice on earth. In the gospels we find that the apostles were given power to do what Jesus did in three ways. They were given the power to teach the truth faithfully. They were given power over the forces of evil, illness and death. They were also given the power to forgive sins in Jesus name.

The Successors of the Apostles

The New Testament book, *The Acts of the Apostles* tells us how these 'sent ones' got on with the job. The story opens with the Day of Pentecost. The apostles were gathered with Mary, the mother of Jesus and Jesus' other followers wondering what would happen next. Suddenly the Holy Spirit came upon them and they received power for the task that Jesus had given them.

Peter - the one Jesus had called 'the Rock' - emerged as their natural leader. He preached to crowds of people about Jesus and thousands responded to the good news, believed in Jesus and were baptised. Eventually a prominent Jew named Paul was converted and joined the apostles. He was the first apostle of the next generation. Through a powerful conversion experience he also claimed to have been chosen by Christ and his calling was confirmed by the other apostles. Together Peter and Paul helped to establish the church. The other apostles went into the whole known world spreading the good news and starting churches wherever they went. Before long, throughout the Roman Empire, little groups of Christians were meeting in homes and local halls. The new little religion prospered and grew. Churches flourished and soon in the major cities there were many little cells of believers in Jesus Christ. The apostles appointed leaders in each city and it was natural for the leader the apostles appointed to become the leader of all the Christians in that city and surrounding area.

Jesus had promised to be with his followers forever, and the first generation of Christians realised that, after the death of the apostles, the power Jesus had given them had been passed on to the church leaders they had appointed. The idea that leadership could be 'handed on' from one leader to the next generation was a normal part of the culture of the day. As a result the leaders of the churches (called bishops) were seen to be the natural successors of the apostles.

Built on the Rock

Saint Paul had said that the church was built on the solid foundation of the prophets and apostles. He must have been thinking of a conversation Jesus had had with Peter. Peter's given name was Simon, but when he recognised that Jesus was actually the Son of God, Jesus responded by praising him and giving him a new name. From then on he was to be called 'Peter' which means 'Rock.' Then Jesus said, 'On this rock I will build my church.'

After he rose from the dead Jesus appointed Peter to the leadership role in a different way. He asked Peter three times to 'feed my sheep.' Jesus had already said that he was the Good Shepherd, and just before he went back to heaven he delegated the Shepherd's job to Peter.

Peter was chosen for his leadership skills and he emerged as the natural leader after Jesus' return to heaven. Eventually he went to Rome and with Paul, founded the church in the Empire's capital city. The leaders of the Roman Church were therefore seen to be the successors of Peter. Because Peter was the leader of the twelve apostles it was natural that his successors - the leaders of the Roman Church - were also seen to be the leaders of the whole church.

Catholics believe that there is still a successor of Peter active in the world today. The present-day Bishop of Rome is the Pope. The word Pope simply means 'Papa.' The Pope is our spiritual father on earth. He speaks today with the same voice of authority that Jesus gave to Peter two thousand years ago.

Reliable Leadership

It is impossible for any organisation to prosper without proper leadership. It is impossible for any army to win a war without a supreme commander. Likewise, the church cannot enjoy unity if it is not united under one leader. Jesus the Good Shepherd said that there would be, 'one flock and one shepherd.' He asked Peter to be that shepherd in his name. We believe Peter's successor still plays the same unifying leadership role today.

The Pope is not an all-powerful absolute monarch. The New Testament shows that Peter ruled by consulting the other apostles and deciding on matters together with them. Likewise, the Pope rules the church through consultation with all the bishops of the world as well as through their consultation with all the priests and people. This is not a democracy. It is a collaborative and consultative council with a clear leader at the top and a clear chain of command.

Jesus promised his followers that the Holy Spirit, the 'Spirit of Truth' would come to them. In this way Jesus guaranteed to his followers a measure of his own ability to teach the truth without error. This same gift resides in the church today. The bishops of the church maintain, defend, develop and teach the same truth that has been handed down to them from the apostles. Because of this historic truth we can rely on the leaders of the Church to teach the truth without error.

Written Answers

The teaching of the Catholic Church is rooted in the faith, life and ministry of the apostles. They were empowered and granted authority by Jesus himself. We believe that the church today teaches with that same authority and is empowered by the same Holy Spirit.

One of the fruits of the Church's power to

understand and teach the truth is the Bible. The Bible is a collection of Jewish and Christian religious writings. The Christians of the first few centuries gathered together the stories of Jesus.

The first Christians also gathered the letters that the apostles had written to the churches. They gathered the history of the apostles' lives and some other writings. Eventually they recognised that the Holy Spirit had actually helped the human authors write these unique witnesses to Jesus Christ.

These writings were then granted special church approval as the Holy Scriptures or the Bible. The Bible then became the unique source book for further teachings. The leaders of the Church realised that the words of the Bible put them in intimate contact with the teachings of the apostles, and therefore with Jesus himself. The Scriptures gave them a firm guideline and measuring rod for the truth. Nothing they could preach or teach could ever contradict the Bible. If it did, they were wrong and not the Bible.

In addition to the written teaching of the apostles there was an unwritten body of teaching. The preachers and teachers of one generation handed down the teachings of the apostles in oral form. This 'tradition' is also a valuable part of the apostolic faith. Because it is an oral tradition it is dynamic and living. The Catholic Church maintains the apostolic tradition as another branch of apostolic teaching alongside the Bible. The fullness of the Christian faith is expressed in the historic, full blooded beliefs of the Catholic Church. These beliefs are presented in the *Catechism of the Catholic Church.* This is a scholarly, readable and inspiring text that draws together the truths of the Bible and the truths of Christian tradition to express clearly what Catholics believe.

The Catechism is a clear collection of Catholic beliefs, but Catholic beliefs are not just book knowledge. The Bible and the oral tradition of the Church are rooted in the living experience of the people of God. The Bible and the tradition complement each other, and come alive as the Bible is read within the daily and weekly worship of the people of God. It is good to read the Bible on our own, but we must always be aware that the Bible on its own can be interpreted in many different ways. Like statistics, it can mean almost anything to anybody. That is why Catholics always read the Bible in the context of the ongoing traditions of the church. In that way, the church that gave us the Bible also helps us to understand the Bible correctly.

Authority without Authoritarianism

As I mentioned earlier an American handbook of religions recently estimated the number of non-Catholic Christian denominations at about 20,000. The reason there are so many different groups is because the leaders of these groups have all disagreed amongst themselves.

They disagree because they have looked only to the Bible as their source book, and they have read the Bible outside the context of the Church. The Bible alone does not have the authority to teach us without error. If it did, then there would not be 20,000 different non-Catholic denominations - each one of which claims to be following the Bible.

When we say that the Catholic faith is 'apostolic' we mean that we follow the faith of the apostles as expressed in the Bible, but we also believe that the Holy Spirit who inspired those apostles is still alive today. That same Spirit works through the teaching ministry of the church. The Pope and the bishops of the church are the successors of the apostles, and they are empowered to teach us how to understand the Christian faith in all its fullness.

When we say the pope is 'infallible' we simply mean that when it comes to matters of faith and morals the pope, as the church's spokesman, has been given the gift to teach us God's way without error. This doesn't mean the pope is a sinless person or that he never makes mistakes in ordinary areas of human opinion. It simply means that when he teaches the simple Christian truths for all Christians we can be confident that he does so reliably and without error.

6. Privileges and Duties

Because the Church is One, Holy, Catholic and Apostolic we have a clear responsibility as members of the Church. As individuals we also have a duty to be One, Holy, Catholic and Apostolic.

These four descriptions of the Church help us to understand our goal and destiny as Christians. To take them in reverse order; I am called as an individual to follow the faith that was first taught by the Apostles and has been handed down to me through the ages.

The Apostolic faith is found in the Bible, but it is also available to me through the continued teaching and preaching of the Church. When you go to Mass the priest gives a homily that helps you to understand how the apostolic faith applies to your life today.

Several times a year the bishop of each diocese issues a pastoral letter that helps maintain, defend and apply the apostolic faith. The pope writes and publishes encyclical letters that also address particular concerns and help to apply the apostolic faith in the world today.

Finally, there is a wealth of Catholic material that helps to teach the apostolic faith. Books, television stations, videos, pamphlets, music and websites all keep the apostolic faith alive and help you understand it and apply it better.

For Better of For Worse

The apostolic faith includes not only the religious truths about Jesus Christ and the Church, but also the teaching on how Christians should live.

Catholics have been blamed in the past for focussing too much on sin and making people feel guilty for what they've done wrong. It is true that some Catholic leaders have done this in a negative way. However, it is part of the Church's duty to show us where we're going wrong just as it is a doctor's duty to diagnose a serious illness correctly.

The doctor diagnoses cancer not because he wants you to die, but because he wants you to get better. It is the same when the Church points out where our lives are going wrong. She has the courage to tell us what is wrong not because she wants us to feel bad, but because she wants us to get better.

Being a Christian means that we are constantly aware of our failings, but it also means we are constantly aware of God's help in our lives. Christians are keenly alert to their failures because they are so keenly alert to how much better life can be.

A Wider Vision

If we are called to follow the apostolic faith as individuals, we are also called to practice a universal faith. Being a Christian is not just about me and God or even about me and God and my local community. It is about me and God and the whole universe.

Being Catholic means that my own little life is put in perspective. My personality, my race, my nationality and background are all part of a much wider family that includes every other race, nationality and background in the world. As such, I am responsible for these other Christians, and they are responsible for me. To be Catholic means that I must get involved in the lives of others.

In my personal life this means that I must respect others sexually. No man or woman can be regarded as mere sex toy. Neither can I exploit or use people by cheating them, stealing from them or abusing them in any way. From now on every person is my brother or my sister.

This worldwide vision of my place in relationship with the whole of humanity affects other aspects of my life too. I must care for the poor, the disabled, the refugees, political prisoners and the oppressed wherever they may be. God may call me to give my life in service to these poor and outcast brothers and sisters of mine, or he may simply enable me to support others who work to help those who are less well off.

I cannot be complacent. My life is no longer my own. It has been given to me in order to help my brothers and sisters in this universal family of God called the Catholic Church.

Be Perfect as Your Father in Heaven is Perfect

Jesus actually told his apostles that they should be perfect as God is perfect. Talk about setting high standards! What he meant by this is that each one of us who are members of the One, Holy, Catholic and Apostolic Church are called not only to follow the apostolic faith, and not only to have a universal outlook, but to strive after real holiness.

Every day of our life should now have a new goal: we are taking a further step towards that wholeness or 'holiness' that God has designed us to attain. This means that every word, action, thought and decision must be focussed to this aim.

This activity is empowered by the Holy Spirit, and the Holy Spirit's power is delivered to us through the ministry of the Church. Once we see that this is the goal then all the other do's and don'ts of religion take their proper place. All the guidelines and commandments that the church gives us are suddenly not the end in themselves, but a means to an end. Likewise, the sacraments of the Church cease to be religious duties and become events in which we receive the power to live the Christian life.

If we are called to be completely holy, then the rules and disciplines of the religious life become as joyful and difficult for us as an athlete's training programme. An athlete doesn't mind getting up early, keeping to a strict diet and a gruelling regime of exercise. He has his eyes set on the goal. He knows what he wants to achieve, and the training is merely the tool to get there.

It is the same in the religious life. To be holy requires discipline in prayer, in self sacrifice, in study and in a constant check on our more selfish instincts. This regime can become legalistic and sour, but it is meant to be as liberating and life giving as the athlete's training. Remember, running a race is exhilarating as well as exhausting, an adventure may be dangerous, but it is also exciting.

That They May Be One

In his last hours Jesus prayed that his followers, 'might be one as you and I Father, are one.' In other words, Jesus wanted them to be one with him, but he also wanted them to be one with each other, and one within themselves.

We follow the apostolic faith, we maintain a universal outlook, we strive and train for holiness because we are seeking this essential unity of being. We want to be one within ourselves. We want to be one with each other. We want to be one with the whole of creation. We want to be one with God.

We begin to share in this unity through our worship in the Catholic Church. We make a commitment to attend Mass every week because that is where we get re-focussed. At Mass the unity we long for actually exists - even if it is still imperfect. At Mass we join ourselves with Christ, we join ourselves with our Christian brothers and sisters and we join ourselves with God. 'Communion' actually means 'union with' or 'union across' and so at Holy Communion or the Mass or The Eucharist, that union that will one day have an eternal dimension starts to live in our lives right now.

Transformation Starts at Home

Staying in touch with Christ, and then spreading his life and love throughout the world lead to a final goal. We are actually called to a higher and greater destiny than any of us can imagine. We are destined to become the very sons and daughters of God. Each one of us, with all our sadness, failures and regrets, are called to total redemption and transformation. Jesus Christ wants us to be made into his likeness and to share the radiance of his glory.

The beautiful thing about the Christian faith is that this glory is not found in the things that appear high and mighty. The glory is found instead in the things that are lowly and humble. The fact that God's son came to be born in a drafty stable says it all. The glory of heaven is always expressed in the simplicity of ordinary life.

Therefore if we want to be transformed into the radiant glory of Christ we don't begin by striving for high and holy religious experiences. We don't attempt great feats of prayer, abstinence and self denial. We don't lock ourselves away pursuing a lofty spiritual existence. Instead we get on with ordinary life in an extraordinary way.

Christ's glory shining out of the ordinary life of a carpenter in Nazareth two thousand years ago reminds us that it is in our ordinary tasks, trials and tribulations that our transformation will be discovered. So be ordinary in an extraordinary way. Connect with Christ in the ordinary, sometimes boring glory of Mass every week. See the chance to be like Christ by getting up early to do the breakfast, helping others even when they didn't ask, and living a life of simple sacrifice every day.

It is by being ourselves that we are transformed beyond ourselves. It is by following Christ in our everyday lives that we become like him, and it is through a lifetime of this simple spiritual life that we are able to transform the whole world.

7. Further Up and Further In

The spiritual way is not the easiest path through life. Jesus said the way was narrow and there were few who find it. On the other hand he said the way to spiritual destruction was a broad downward slope. It is easy to slide into hell. It is difficult to climb into heaven.

Is anything good ever easy? What great thing has ever been done overnight? It is true that we are called to a glory beyond our imagining. It is true that we are called to be radiant and everlasting beings - no less than sons and daughters of God himself. But it is also true that we have a long way to go.

But when you think about it, is there really anything else worth living for? Physical pleasure fades. Money is only good in this life. They don't put pockets in shrouds. Status and fame disappear. All those who remember you also die. Even our dearest human loves will be snatched away by illness and death. Our only hope is to be united with all that we love in a greater reality beyond the grave.

The spiritual life therefore not only leads to a happier existence here, but it offers the only hope for a happier existence on the other side of death.

That happy existence is not guaranteed simply because we happen to want it.

Jesus Christ has opened up the way to eternal life. He has given it to us as a free gift, but that treasure must be sought for and found. The treasure is free, but we must study the map and go on the long journey to find it. Living our lives for this end is the best investment anyone can ever make.

Moving Further Up and Further Into God's Glory

The glorious thing about following the spiritual path is that every day we are making further progress towards all that we have ever loved and longed for in life. Every path leads somewhere, and if we are following the way of Christ, then he is not only the way, he is also the destination.

Heaven is not simply a happy place on the other side of the clouds where we will see all our loved ones once again. Heaven is the fulfilment of all our hopes and dreams. It is a reality that makes everything on this earth seem like a dream.

Some people say you make your own heaven and hell here on earth. This is true in one sense, but it is more true to say that you are choosing between heaven or hell every day here on earth. You are choosing heaven or hell because every day - indeed every moment - you are choosing whether you wish to live God's way or your way. If you wish to live God's way, then that way will logically lead to God. If you choose to live your way, then your choice naturally leads away from God.

To choose heaven therefore, is not a once and for all choice. It is an each and every day choice. Will we choose to connect with Jesus at Mass and confession, or will we ignore him? Will we choose to give our money and time to a Christian cause or will we spend time for our own pleasure? Will we give of ourselves for the good of others or simply pursue our own desires? Down one route lies heaven. Down the other lies hell.

The Slippery Slope

Is there such a place as hell? Will people really be tormented forever with pain and fire? Hell is a spiritual condition, not a physical place. But in saying that, the spiritual realm is not less real than this world, but more real. If this is so, then to say it that hell is a 'spiritual realm' is not to say hell is unreal. Instead, hell is more real than we can imagine, even though that reality is of a different dimension.

It is not pleasant to think about hell, but when you do think about it, it becomes clear that hell is a necessity. If heaven is a place of goodness and justice, then there must be a place for all those who, all their lives, have run from all that is good, true and just.

Does God send people to hell? It is more likely that he simply gives each of us what we always wanted. If some people flee from goodness, truth and beauty all their lives can we imagine that they would actually want to go to heaven - the place where goodness, truth and beauty are written into every atom and morsel of reality? They would flee from such goodness, and the place they would prefer must be hell.

Perhaps then it is simply the case that the light of God is the same light to those who are saved and those who are damned. The only difference is that for those who have always loved goodness, truth and beauty the light will be the light of Christ, while for those who have always loved evil the same light will be experienced as the searing flames of hell.

Whatever hell consists of, we can say that it must be the everlasting torture of being left alone without God, without love, without beauty, without goodness and without truth. If we have choice, then we must have the choice to go there. If we do any action that, by its very nature, takes us away from God, and if we persist in that action without ever acknowledging that we are wrong, we are in danger of ending up with the fruit of that action - and that fruit is a future cut off from God, from life and from love.

The Third Way

Talking about heaven and hell in such black and white terms makes people uncomfortable. In one sense there is nothing wrong with that. Hell is meant to be uncomfortable, and the best sermon ever preached about hell consists of only two words: 'Fear Hell.'

But people are also uncomfortable because we all realise that things are not so black and white. Each one of us might long for heaven, but we also stumble and fall into our darker desires, laziness and selfishness. The eternal state of each one of our hearts is not so clear cut.

If we are honest we admit that we are not saintly enough to go straight to heaven, but we also hope that we are not wicked enough to head for hell. To see ourselves this way is not proud or unduly humble. It is just realistic.

This is why the church teaches that there is a place called 'purgatory'. 'Purgatory' simply means a place of purgation or cleansing. Everybody in purgatory will eventually make it to heaven. It's just that they need some time to get their act together. If you like, purgatory is a place to wash up before mealtime. It is a place where our failures, imperfections and faults can continue to be put right by the help of God's gift of grace. As long as we have sought God's way in this life; as long as we have put our trust in Christ's saving work, we can have a confident hope that after a time being cleaned up we will enter into the final glory of God's presence.

All Shall be Well

This final hope is the glory and joy of all Christians. We do not simply wish for pie in the sky and a happy hunting ground after we pass on. Instead heaven is the fulfilment of all things in heaven and earth. There all that is divided shall be one. There all that was soiled and impure shall be holy and wholly itself. There all that was small and narrow minded will be universal in its scope and vision.

The vision of heaven in the New Testament has the apostles and prophets on thrones around the throne of God. This is a symbolic way of saying that heaven will be a fulfilment of all that the church hints at here on earth. The welcome home we receive when we become Catholics is just a hint of the greater welcome home we shall receive on entry into heaven.

Heaven will be like a great family reunion, or a vast wedding feast. Everyone will be gathered in the unity and peace for which they were created. At that point the transformation of every soul will be complete. Each one of us will be fully and wholly ourselves because we have found our rightful place in the everlasting life of Christ.

At that point all that confused and distressed us will be seen as part of a much larger pattern. Then our cloudy vision will clear and we will see that we fit into a destiny for the universe that was far more wonderful and beautiful than we ever could have imagined. We will understand that every detail of our lives was a step toward this place and that we have arrived home and know the place for the first time.

Additional Reading

The New Testament
The Catechism of the Catholic Church

Christian Classics

Mere Christianity by C.S. Lewis
The Screwtape Letters by C.S. Lewis
Orthodoxy by G.K. Chesterton
The Everlasting Man by G.K. Chesterton
The Creed in Slow Motion by Ronald Knox
Early Christian Writings by Maxwell Staniforth
The Penguin Dictionary of Saints by Donald Attwater
and Catherine Rachel Jones

Modern Catholic Books

Catholic Lives by Greg Watts - a collection of stories
of people who have become Catholic.

The Path to Rome by Dwight Longenecker - a more
weighty collection of conversion stories than
Catholic Lives.

More Christianity by Dwight Longenecker - this book
explains the Catholic faith in a friendly way to non-
Catholic Christians.

Adventures in Orthodoxy by Dwight Longenecker - a witty and colourful exploration of Christian belief.

Exploring the Catholic Church by Marcellino D'Ambrosio - a good small introduction to the Catholic Church today.

What Catholics Really Believe by Karl Keating - exploration of the Catholic faith in a question and answer format.

Knowing the Real Jesus by David Mills - a well written exploration of what the first Christians thought about Jesus Christ.

Surprised by Truth by Patrick Madrid - three volumes of American conversion stories.

Where is that in the Bible? and *Where is that in Tradition?* by Patrick Madrid - easy to read Catholic answers written in a punchy style.

What to do next...

You can order one or all of the other books in the CTS Christianity Pure & Simple series:

1. Is Anybody There? (Ref Do 699)

2. The God Man (Ref Do 700)

3. The Fire Of Life (Ref Do 701)

4. The Great Battle (Ref Do 702)

5. Welcome Home (Ref Do 703)

The quickest way to order is to call CTS direct on 020 7640 0042

You can send us a fax if you wish, on 020 7640 0046

Or pop your order in the post to:
CTS, 40-46 Harleyford Road,
Vauxhall, London SE11 5AY

Or visit our website
www.cts-online.org.uk/pureandsimple.htm

If this book has interested you and you want to discover more about Christianity then you may also find useful the following list of organisations:

www.faithcafe.org

If perhaps you already have some familiarity with the Catholic Church, but would like to explore some of the themes you've read about in this series, your local church may run Catholic Faith Exploration or CaFE

Catholic Enquiry Office

For enquiries about becoming a Catholic, knowing more about the Church or finding your local parish church. 114 West Heath Road, London NW3 7TX; Tel: 020 8458 3316; Email: ceo@cms.org.uk